PENNIES

BY MADDIE SPALDING

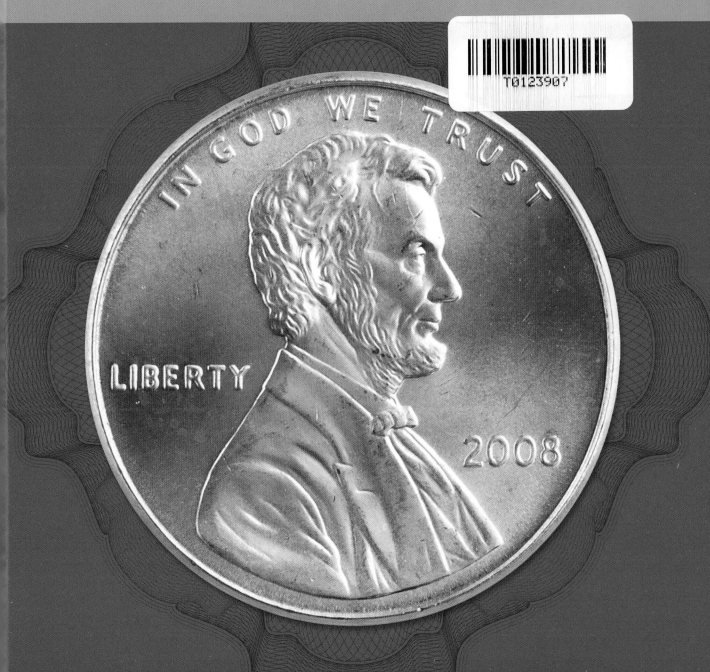

The Child's World®
childsworld.com

Published by The Child's World®
1980 Lookout Drive • Mankato, MN 56003-1705
800-599-READ • www.childsworld.com

Photographs ©: Shutterstock Images, cover, 1, 5 (top); iStockphoto,
5 (bottom), 11, 19, 20 (top), 20 (middle); JMB Studio/iStockphoto,
5, 6; Roman Babakin/Shutterstock Images, 9; Everett Historical/
Shutterstock Images, 13; James Pintar/Shutterstock Images,
15; Melinda Fawver/Shutterstock Images, 16–17; Peter Spiro/
iStockphoto, 20 (bottom); Red Line Editorial, 22

Design Elements: JMB Studio/iStockphoto; Ben Hodosi/
Shutterstock Images

ISBN 9781503820012
LCCN 2016960500

Printed in the United States of America
PA02336

ABOUT THE AUTHOR

Maddie Spalding writes and edits children's books. She lives in Minnesota.

TABLE OF CONTENTS

CHAPTER ONE

WHAT IS A PENNY?

Pennies are U.S. coins. They are worth one cent. One penny can be written 1¢ or $0.01. Twenty-five pennies make one quarter. One hundred pennies make one dollar.

How is a penny different from a dollar bill?

Five pennies make one nickel.

Abraham Lincoln

Year the coin was made

Abraham Lincoln is on the front of the penny.

"E Pluribus Unum" is the United States motto. It is Latin for "Out of Many, One."

Union Shield

A shield is on the back of the penny.

CHAPTER TWO

THE HISTORY OF THE PENNY

The United States Mint makes coins. The U.S. Mint is part of the U.S. government. It was created in 1792. The first U.S. pennies were **minted** that year.

One United States Mint location is in Philadelphia, Pennsylvania.

A woman was on the front of the first U.S. pennies. Her name was Lady Liberty. The penny **design** changed many times. Some older pennies have eagles. Others show Lady Liberty wearing a Native American headdress.

This penny from 1899 shows Lady Liberty
wearing a Native American headdress.

Abraham Lincoln was put on the penny in 1909. It was the 100-year **anniversary** of his birth. President Theodore Roosevelt wanted to show him respect.

Why might Theodore Roosevelt have wanted to show respect for Abraham Lincoln?

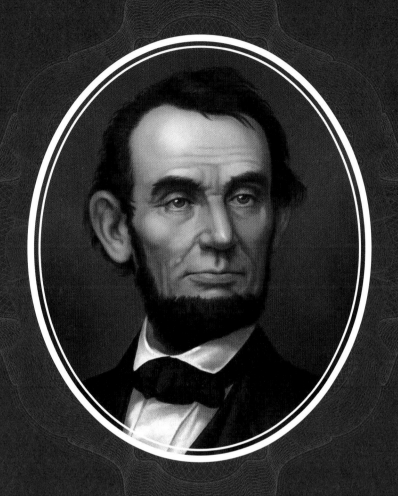

ABRAHAM LINCOLN

was the 16th president of the United States (1861–1865). He led the country during the U.S. Civil War.

CHAPTER THREE

MAKING A PENNY

Pennies are made from zinc. They are coated in copper. Zinc and copper are metals.

Copper is a metal. Pennies are coated in copper.

At the U.S. Mint,
machines cut metal
into **discs**. A coin press
stamps designs on
the discs.

Each penny is stamped by a coin press. This creates the penny's design.

The U.S. Mint sends pennies to banks. Pennies travel all over the country. Each penny has its own history.

Why do you think some people collect coins?

Pennies and other coins trade hands with people from all over the United States.

1853 U.S. penny

1792 The first U.S. penny was minted.

1859 The front of the penny changed to Lady Liberty wearing a Native American headdress.

1899 U.S. penny

1909 Abraham Lincoln first appeared on the penny.

2009 The U.S. Mint made new penny designs to honor the 200-year anniversary of Lincoln's birth.

2009 U.S. penny

★ An original 1792 U.S. penny is expensive today. In 2015, someone paid nearly $2.6 million for one.

★ Pennies cost more to make than what they are worth. It costs about 1.8 cents to make one U.S. penny.

★ The U.S. Mint makes about 30 million pennies per day.

★ Some countries used to have pennies but do not anymore. Canada stopped making pennies in 2012.

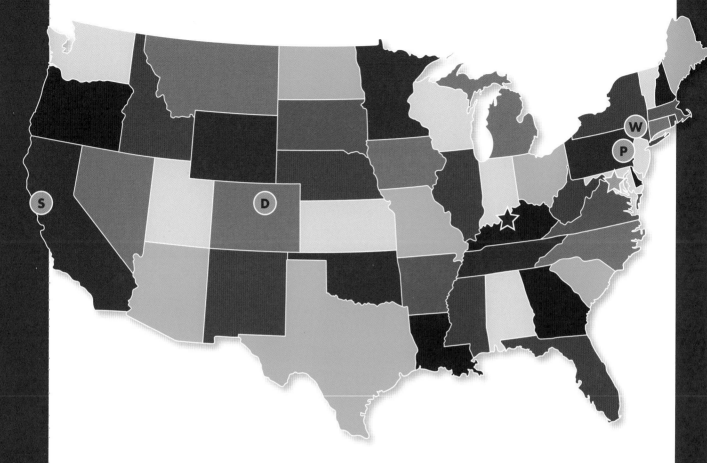

KEY

⭐ Fort Knox, Kentucky—Storage of U.S. gold

⭐ Washington, DC—Headquarters of the U.S. Mint

COIN-PRODUCING MINTS

D Denver, Colorado—Produces coins marked with a D.

P Philadelphia, Pennsylvania—Produces coins marked with a P.

S San Francisco, California—Produces coins marked with an S.

W West Point, New York—Produces coins marked with a W.

anniversary (an-uh-VUR-suh-ree): An anniversary is a date where something important happened. Abraham Lincoln was put on the penny for the anniversary of his birth.

design (di-ZINE): A design is the style of something. The U.S. penny design has changed many times.

discs (DISKS): Discs are flat, circular objects. Metal discs are used to make coins.

minted (MINT-ed): A coin that is minted is made out of metal. U.S. pennies were minted in 1792.

IN THE LIBRARY

Dowdy, Penny. *Money*. New York, NY: Crabtree, 2009.

Fitzgerald, Lee. *Pennies!* New York, NY: PowerKids, 2016.

Gilpin, Caroline Crosson. *Abraham Lincoln*. Washington, DC: National Geographic, 2012.

Williams, Rozanne Lanczak. *The Coin Counting Book*. Watertown, MA: Charlesbridge, 2011.

ON THE WEB

Visit our Web site for links about pennies: childsworld.com/links

Note to Parents, Teachers, and Librarians: We routinely verify our Web links to make sure they are safe and active sites. So encourage your readers to check them out!

INDEX